COMMUNICATION

FROM

HIS HONOR THE MAYOR,

FERNANDO WOOD,

TRANSMITTED TO THE COMMON COUNCIL OF NEW-YORK,

JULY 7TH, 1856.

NEW-YORK:
1856.

COMMUNICATION

FROM

HIS HONOR THE MAYOR,

FERNANDO WOOD,

TRANSMITTED TO THE COMMON COUNCIL
OF NEW-YORK,

JULY 7TH, 1856.

NEW-YORK:
1856.

MAYOR'S OFFICE,
NEW-YORK, July 7th, 1856.

To the Honorable the Common Council:

GENTLEMEN—In the several communications which I have had the honor to address to the Common Council since my incumbency of the office of Mayor, I have endeavored to present subjects for consideration of importance to the welfare and prosperity of the city. It has been my aim to fully carry out the requirements of the charter, which makes it the duty of the Mayor to recommend for the adoption of the Common Council all such measures as are for the advancement of the interests of the people.

In these several messages I have covered a wide field for legislative action, and though but few of the topics treated of have been favorably received, yet I am constrained to believe that seed has been sown, which will not prove entirely barren. The fruit will appear in good time, and long after the hand which pens these lines has lost its vitality these suggestions will be received and adopted, and their merits acknowledged and appreciated.

I now propose to present a topic of probably greater moment than any which has preceeded it, and which, if adopted, will raise the City still higher as the object of national pride.

I allude to the establishment by the Corporation of a great University, for the purposes of imparting the very highest order of education, not now to be obtained in this country, and to be free and open to all who will partake of its advantages.

This proposition may at first be startling to those who may think they see in it enormous additions to our already heavy taxes ; but I am confident that a careful perusal of this document and just appreciation of the subject will dispel such fears, and show that whilst no great additional expenditure will be required, the return in all the solid advantages of public and individual wealth will re-pay ten fold, any outlay in consequence.

It is a mistake to suppose the State, represented to the people of this City by the local authorities, has fulfilled its highest functions when it has afforded protection to life, liberty and property. Men may live in safety and freedom, and in the secure enjoyment of wealth, and yet live to little purpose. Life, liberty and property have their just value in opening the possibilities and means of reaching those noble ends, which are found in the development of their intelligent and moral being. It is not enough to live, but to live wisely and honestly ; not enough to be free, but to make a proper use of freedom ; not enough to possess property, but to know how to appreciate it in order to gain the greatest amount of good. Hence it is required of the State that it shall provide a system of education, whereby knowledge shall be diffused as widely as possible, and the means of generous culture and refinement be offered in every degree. Were it possible without the means of knowledge and culture to improve our internal condition and circumstances, still without these we could not hold the proper rank and privileges of men, and the powers of government would be exercised without an adequate object. But in addition to this it is evident that to maintain a position among the civilized nations, and to *possess* the wealth, power and advantages which belong to such nations, a system of public education is indispensible. This fact was well known to and appreciated by the enlightened and enterprizing citizens who first suggested the Free Academy for this city, which though but partially supplying our wants, is an institution of great merit.

The distinguished characteristic of Democratical Institutions, as well as their highest glory, is that whatever is necessary to the welfare of man, whatever is calculated to exalt his nature, to enlarge the sphere of his usefulness, to multiply and refine his enjoyments, to give dignity to his position—in fine, whatever goes to develope him to what God and nature designed him to be—is made possible to the whole people. The rights of life, liberty, opinion, property, religion, education and the pursuit of happiness are secured alike to all.

Among these, there is no more important, no dearer right than that of EDUCATION. Indeed, this is necessary to the proper enjoyment of all the others. With education, involving as it does an acquaintance with science and the arts, is connected all advance in manufactories, commerce and mechanical inventions. The savage has these only in the rudest and most imperfect state, because he is uneducated. The civilized man has them in a more perfected state, only because he is educated. Education is the foundation of all material prosperity, and national wealth and power. But beyond this, education gives birth to social elevation, and refinement; to the capacity of political self-government, and to all those humane arts which give man his true rank, and make his existence valuable and important. Religion and morals depend no less upon education, and by it alone are we elevated above a degrading superstition, and mere prejudice and custom, to an intelligent worship of God, and a proper knowledge of human duties in all human relations. We may lay it down, therefore, it is an indisputable axiom, that the highest duty of the State is to provide for the adequate education of the people. This is true under all forms of government—it is pre-eminently true under a Democratic government.

We have, indeed, accepted this axiom, so far as Common Schools are concerned. But the question may be asked, why should it be confined to Common Schools? Do Common Schools provide for all the wants of the people? By no means. In the first place, Common Schools cannot provide teachers for Common Schools; and so we need a higher grade of institutions to provide them; and we have actually advanced upon this idea, in the creation of Normal Schools and the Free Academy, and from these must come teachers for the Common Schools. But again, the Normal Schools and the Free Academy do not furnish teachers for themselves, but they must be obtained from still higher institutions. Thus it is plain, that for the protection of the lowest grade of education, we must run back to institutions where ripe and finished scholars in the different branches of knowledge are made. To carry out popular education properly and efficiently, we want a system of institutions where the higher fosters the lower, and where scholars of the lower may advance step by step to the higher. It is a mistaken idea, that the Common Schools are the only popular institutions. Every institution is popular which is freely laid open to the people. The people have a right, not only to Common School education, but to every grade of education to which any of them may aspire. We repudiate the doctrine as anti-democratical in the highest degree, that the higher forms of education belong only to the rich and privileged classes. To a free people every degree of education should be possible. The poor man as well as the rich should have the privilege of educating his son, as a clergyman, a physician, a lawyer, a civil engineer, a teacher or professor, or a man of science. Men of the most distinguished eminence have come up from the poorer classes; but then they have come up struggling through manifold difficulties and hindrances ; while multitudes have been left in ignorance and obscurity whose capacities might have been unfolded to the highest standard of humanity, had they only enjoyed opportunities of education. The sons of rich men often pass through the mere forms of education, only to neglect and abuse their privileges. The sons of poor men are more likely to value them. We have had enough of the martyrdom of struggling talent and genius in our world. It should be the glory of a country like ours, to put an end to it, by creating for the people institutions where poor men, as well as rich may gain any degree of knowledge they please. Indeed, scholars springing up on all sides from among the poorer classes would stimulate the sons of the rich, and instead of resigning themselves to mediocrity, imbecility, or ruinous dissipation, they would find it necessary in the higher tone of society which would be created, to exert themselves to gain those manly and intellectual accomplishments which become necessary to respectability and influence. Poor men, too, would become elevated by the very ambition of educating their children, and through the influence which their education would reflect back upon them. In this way degradation and vice would be gradually removed and subdued, intelligence and morality be diffused, and a spirit of good order created more potent to put down excesses, restrain crime, and to throw protection around our homes, than the most numerous and best disciplined police.

No country requires as many men of high education as ours. This appears both from the fact, that numerous forms of business which require intelligence, are open to all the people, and the fact that all the people are eligible to political offices. And in connection with this fact, of the general eligibility to political office, we must take into consideration the rotation of office, which imposes the necessity of a greater number of well qualified men than where office is held permanently by one set of men.

The political evils which we now labor under arise from this very want of the wide diffusion of the higher degrees of education among the people. Knowledge is power, and did they possess it as they are entitled to, the land would never be under the dominion of ignorant and unprincipled demagogues, who often prevail by brute cunning and violence.

In view, then, of all this, and of much more which might be said on this all important subject, it behooves us to look carefully at our system of public education and to inquire, what yet remains to be done to give the people in full, the opportunites and privileges of education in the largest sense.

It must be obvious to all, in the first place, that an Institution similar to the Free Academy ought to be established for the education of females. At present no provision is made by the State for the education of the other sex save that which is found in the Primary Schools. Any higher degree of Education can be obtained only at private establishments, which are so expensive as to preclude, absolutely, the daughters of poor men, and of those of moderate means. An Institution for the higher education of females ought, indeed, to be ordered differently from the Free Academy. The Ancient Classics and the higher Mathematics, for examaple, would not be required. But a knowledge of all the Sciences to a certain extent, of History, of Moral Science, of Belles-lettres, of the English language and Literature, of Music and Drawing, and in general of whatever contributes to tasteful culture, and to that refinement and elevation of character, which give a proper charm and influence to the sex, ought to be provided for. Such an Institution is most important as affording protection to morals and diffusing among the people a finer tone of feelings. The daughters of the people, in turn, become the mothers of the people and govern the very heart of society.

In the next place, it is no less obvious that one Free Academy which we now have, must very soon prove inadequate to the wants of the young men of this city, and other institutions of the same kind, will need to be established. This Institution symbolizes more and more to the European Schools, known as Gymnasia. Now, the city of Berlin alone, with half the population of New York, maintains seven of these Schools, containing together about three thousand five hundred pupils, where those who are able to pay, pay about sixteen dollars a year, and where those who are unable to pay are educated gratuitously. The Democratic City of New York ought not to be behind the despotic city of Berlin.

But the free academies and every grade of School, require at this moment, most of all for their successful multiplication and development, the presence of the highest grade of educational instruction. Such an Institution would educate teachers of the highest grade, who would educate teachers of a lower grade. That is, the University would educate teachers for the Free Academies and Normal Schools; and the Free Academies and Normal Schools would educate teachers for all the subordinate grades. Thus would our system be completed and maintained in healthful action. The creation of the University at once, would by its necessary influence and provisions call all the others into being. But, beside this, the University would do just that which I have before indicated as a popular right. It would afford the means of the highest education to all the sons of the people who felt disposed to attempt it. Here in the University we could collect books and apparatus, establish museums and galleries of Art, and call together eminent scholars in every branch of knowledge, to give lectures on the principles, and the practical details and applications of science. The free academies would furnish students for the University, as the University would furnish teachers for the free academies. Students would also flock to the University from the different colleges of our country after graduating there. The two hundred now found in foreign Universities would thus be provided for at home. The number of University students would be increased by the very fact that there would be a University to receive them. The passion for attending the lectures of itinerant lecturers in the community, generally, proves conclusively, that many persons besides the regular students of the University, would be inclined to attend the lectures of the Professors in branches for which they might have a predeliction. This, indeed, is the case in European cities where universities exist. It is evident that a taste for knowledge and self-cultivation, would thus prevail more and more, and our society be animated by an intellectual and tasteful life.

New York, now our Commercial Emporium, would thus become the great seat of learning and the Arts; and would, like Paris and other European Cities, attract multitudes by the charms of its literary advantages, and its all-pervading refinement.

It is humiliating to reflect how generally the great Cities of Europe are the seats of Universities, of Museums and of Galleries of Art, while we remain a mere city of traders. We pay enormous taxes, and get in return material benefits. The people have a right to demand something more than this. Were I treating this subject merely as a political economist, I might say, that it would add vastly to our wealth, and might adduce Paris and Munich as examples.

Now, Americans, after having made their wealth in New York resort to European cities, for what New York might itself be made to afford them, did we make the same provision for intellectual and tasteful cultivation.

For an object of such paramount and vital moment the cost would be comparatively inconsiderable; especially if existing Institutions of learning were made adjuncts, and yet the cost whatever it would be, should be deemed of minor consideration in view of the lasting benefits to be derived.

The cost of the introduction of the Croton Water appalled many at first; but who now counts the cost, while daily and hourly experiencing the blessings of that great work. What the people now ask for is the introduction into the city of a purer and more vital stream—the stream of Knowledge full and overflowing, brought to every man's door, and offered to every man's taste.

It would be the crowning work of our generation, and connect us with all future generations in grateful and honored remembrances. With these views, and deeply impressed with this great National want of such an Institution, I propose that the Corporation establish the University and Academy of Science and Arts of the City of New York, as well as a Free Academy for Females.

In my judgment, the people demand these as the culminating part of a system of public education not now perfected. The great University I propose is just as naturally and properly the work of the City, as the Primary Schools and the existing Free Academy. If the City provides for the rudimentary part of education in the first, and for the disciplining part in the second, why should it not provide for that higher part to which the first look, and only in which case, they reach their proper end. If the city provides for a common business education, why should it not also provide for making scholars and men of science for carrying on those higher investigations and disseminating and applying those higher principles of knowledge, which give birth to all forms of knowledge and lie at the foundation of all industrial and commercial prosperity—of all social education and refinement, and of all political order and security.

But while it is properly the work of the city, such is the nature of a University, and so rich and magnificent are the particulars of which it is composed—consisting of Libraries, Museums, Laboratories, an Observatory, Galleries of Art and Professorships, that it both admits of and invites the co-operation of wealthy individuals devoted to public good and embraces cordially all private undertakings, working towards the same end.

As a grand system, it must belong to the public; but as a work to be performed, every one so disposed may lend his aid to it.

In our City, several things have already been done, both by the public, and by private individuals, which tend towards the realization of this plan. To the first belong the Public Schools and the Free Academy, which more and more conformed to the great end, naturally lead to it, and become necessary to its realization. The great success of our educational system in these institutions gives assured promise of what we may expect, when we undertake that which is to be complete and crown the whole.

Of private efforts, I would call attention particularly to two.

The first is the Astor Library. This library established by the munificent bequest of the late Mr. Astor, and about to be enlarged by the liberality of his son, is already the largest and most valuable labrary in our country, and must, ere long, take its place among the great libraries of the world.

By the will of Mr. Astor, the said Library is designated "a Public Library in the City of New York," and "is to be accessible at all reasonable hours and times, for general use, free of expense to the persons resorting thereto, subject only to such control and regulations, as the trustees may from time to time exercise and establish for general convenience."

By the terms of the bequest, therefore, it becomes available to a University, whenever it shall be established. And unqestionably the trustees, as well as the present Mr. Astor, would regard it as a most happy and honorable destination of this great Library, to become associated with a great University. The second, is the noble appropriation of Mr. Peter Cooper of nearly or quite half a million of dollars to the founding of a Scientific Institution.

Mr. Cooper's plan, as far as developed, plainly aims at objects embraced by a University. I cannot but indulge the hope, therefore, that if invited by the City, he would unite his benefaction with an appropriation from the City, and thus found the most magnificent institution of learning ever attempted in our country. Let this Institution be once founded under a form and with guarantees of its character, to secure the attention and confidence of thinking and philanthropic men, and the means will not be wanting to complete all its parts. Men will become ambitious of giving their names to libraries, museums, galleries of art, observatories and professorships—those noblest of all monuments, because connected with the highest benefits which can be handed down to posterity ; and the most enduring, because they create their own safe-guards, in the spirit which they are ever diffusing, and make their preservation the common interest of mankind.

It is a most encouraging fact that the leading scientific and literary men of our own country, have long been looking earnestly for this great movement ; and that they express a unanimous opinion, both as to its immense importance, and its feasibility.

Whatever doubts may exist, must soon be removed ; whatever opposition may be encountered must soon subside. Notwithstanding all doubt and opposition, the Free Academy is completely successful, and, now, universally popular. Notwithstanding all doubt and opposition, the Croton water now flows into every dwelling, blessing alike the rich and poor—a boon which none would part with, and to be deprived of which a calamity which none dare even to imagine.

Notwithstanding the opposition to the Central Park, long and persistent, it is now a fixed fact, and its necessity universally conceded.

Let this great fountain of knowledge then be opened, also to send its streams into every dwelling. It will carry with it its own vindication, and we will only wonder that we could have been so long contented to be without it. The experience of a good, ends all discussion as to its value and importance.

I am aware that it will be said that this subject more properly belongs to the Board of Education. Whilst admitting that the whole subject of public education is more directly under the control of that Board, it must not be forgotten that that Board occupies relations to the City Government somewhat in the nature of a public Department, and hence that you may appropriately indicate, by legislation, an enlargement of its sphere of action.

If the Board of Education will take up this subject, and carry out these recommendations, so vitally associated with the further progress of the City and of the Country, I shall be most happy, and certainly shall facilitate rather than impede its accomplishment of the object.

It has been said that the Board has ample power for this purpose, without additional legislation. If this be so, I hope you will refer these suggestions at once to that Board, with a recommendation that early and favorable action be taken thereon.

FERNANDO WOOD, *Mayor.*

www.ingramcontent.com/pod-product-compliance
Lightning Source LLC
LaVergne TN
LVHW020639110826
845149LV00004B/1283

* 9 7 8 1 4 1 8 1 9 0 8 2 8 *